Birmingham Repertory Theatre Company
presents

by
Korky Paul and **Valerie Thomas**

Adapted for the stage by
Anthony Clark

Book and Lyrics by **Anthony Clark**

Original Music by **Mark Vibrans**

First performed at
Birmingham Repertory Theatre on
7 December 2001

Winnie the Witch

by **Korky Paul** and **Valerie Thomas**

Book and Lyrics by **Anthony Clark**

Original Music by **Mark Vibrans**

Wilbur the Cat **Mak Wilson**
Winnie the Witch **Elizabeth Marsh**
Ice Cream Seller **Philip Bateman**
Optician **Kelly O'Leary**
Dead-Eyed Pirate Paul **Nicholas Tigg**
All other parts played by the Company

Director **Anthony Clark**
Designer **Rachel Blues**
Lighting **Tim Mitchell** and **Symon Harner**
Musical Director **Philip Bateman**
Puppets made by **Craig Denston**

Stage Manager **Richard Greville Watson**
Deputy Stage Manager **Ruth Morgan**
Assistant Stage Manager **Louise Matthews**

Set built and painted by Birmingham Repertory Theatre
Sound by Birmingham Repertory Theatre
Costumes by Birmingham Repertory Theatre

Birmingham Repertory Theatre
Broad Street
Birmingham B1 2EP
Admin: 0121 245 2000
Fax: 0121 245 2100
Box Office: 0121 236 4455
www.birmingham-rep.co.uk

THE COMPANY

Philip Bateman
Ice Cream Seller and Musical Director

Philip grew up in Camberley, Surrey and studied Music and Drama at Birmingham University.

His work as a Musical Director includes: Workshop for the new *Madness Musical* (Tiger Aspect); *Wild Wild Women* (Orange Tree); *Return to the Forbidden Planet* (National Tour); *A Grand Night for Singing* (Grace Theatre and East Africa Tour); *From a Jack to a King* (Wimbledon Studio) and *Newsrevue* (Canal Café Theatre).

As an actor he has taken the lead role in glam-rock musical *Electric Lipstick* (National Tour); *Pirate Jenny* (Basingstoke Haymarket); *Canterbury Tales* (National Tour with Brian Glover); *Cabaret* (The Watermill, Newbury); *Treasure Island* (National Tour) and Ayckbourn/Todd's *Between The Lines* (Wimbledon Studio).

Philip has been resident pianist on GMTV and singer/keyboard player in *The Breakfast Boys*, the weekly house band on ITV's Lorraine Live. He was also pianist and composer for Channel 4's *Bodystory 2* earlier this year.

Composition: Incidental music for *The Clandestine Marriage* (Watermill, Newbury); *La Maison Suspendue* (RSC at The Other Place); *Faithful Dealing* (Soho Theatre) and *Measure for Measure* (Finborough). Full scores for national tours of *Wheels on the Bus* (based on new TV animation for ATP) and *Polka Dot Shorts* (based on BBC2 TV series) both with writing partner Mark Crossland, and the full score for *Sleeping Beauty* (Proteus Theatre Company).

Elizabeth Marsh
Winnie The Witch

Elizabeth trained at the Guildford School of Acting. She has performed in the West End and at various repertory theatres around the country including the Watermill, Newbury; Theatre Royal, York; City Arts Theatre, Belfast and Queen's Theatre, Hornchurch.

Favourite roles include Annie Wilkes in *Misery*; Beverly in *Abigail's Party*; Jean Rice in *The Entertainer*; Rose in *Brighton Rock*; Louisa in *Hard Times*; Suzanne in *Don't Dress for Dinner*; Rita in *In the Midnight Hour*; Felicity in *Habeus Corpus*; Rapunzel and Florinda in *Into the Woods*; Fay in *A Chorus of Disapproval*; Elizabeth in *Moll Flanders*; Witch in *From a Jack to a King*; Mme Giry in *Phantom of the Opera;* Mrs Kay in *Our Day Out*; Pamela in

The 39 Steps; Fabia in *Twelfth Night* and Yitzak in *Hedwig and the Angry Inch*.

She has also worked as a choreographer on numerous musicals, pantomimes and revues.

Elizabeth has just finished a successful West End run as Cassilda in the critically acclaimed *Gondoliers* at the Apollo Theatre, Shaftesbury Avenue.

Kelly O'Leary
Optician

Kelly was born in Hampshire and trained at Liverpool Institute for Performing Arts.

Her theatre credits include *The Beautiful Game* for Cambridge Theatre where she was understudy, Mary and Christine; Kim in *Daydream Believer* and Laura Ross in *From A Jack to a King,* both for The Gatehouse Theatre; Eileen in *Walking on Sunshine* No.1 Tour, and a repertory season for Wigan Pier Theatre Company. She was also part of the original Cast Recording of *The Beautiful Game*. Kelly has sung at Buckingham Palace for HRH The Queen, Prince Philip, Tony and Cherie Blair.

Nicholas Tigg
Dead-Eyed Pirate Paul

Nicholas was born in London and studied English at University College, London.

He is a founder member of London Small Theatre Company with whom he has toured Europe and America performing Aristophanes' *The Frogs* and *The Clouds*. He has also appeared in *The Frogs* and *Oh! What A Lovely War* for the National Theatre and *Volpone* and *Antony and Cleoptra* for the RSC. Nicholas worked with Ken Campbell on *The Warp*, the world's longest play, providing music for much of the 29 hours, and is a member of and works regularly with *The People Show*, appearing in shows 99, 102, 104 and the recent *Boat Show*. He is a founder member of the National Theatre of Bergamo with whom he is currently devising a new production.

Mak Wilson
Wilbur The Cat

Mak was born in Consett in County Durham and trained at National Youth Theatre and Cannon Hill Puppet Theatre. He first performed at the age of 15 in *Hamlet* at Playhouse Theatre, Newcastle and has since appeared in national tours of *Pinocchio* and *Paddington Bear,* playing the title roles. Other tours include: *The Wizard of Oz, The Wind in the Willows, Happy*

as a *Sandbag* and *Tiger Peter*. Mak first performed puppets with Caricature Theatre, Cardiff in 1978 followed by two and a half years at Cannon Hill Puppet Theatre, Birmingham.

Television credits include: Principal puppeteer on *Spitting Image*; Face Puppeteer of Earl in Henson/Disney's *Dinosaurs*; Mupatop in Henson/CITV's *Mupatops Shop*; Puppeteer and voices of Scooch and Lug in Henson's *Construction Site*.

Mak has worked on fifteen feature films including Plant puppeteer in *The Little Shop of Horrors*; Hoggle puppeteer and several characters in *Labyrinth*; *Who Framed Roger Rabbit?*; Michaelangelo in *Ninja Turtles I & II; Lost in Space*; Puppeteer of Babe in *Babe; Return to Oz; The Bear*.

Anthony Clark
Director/Writer

Anthony started his career in 1981 as Arts Council Assistant Director at The Orange Tree Theatre, directing everything from a school's tour of *Macbeth* to Martin Crimp's first play *Living Remains*. In 1983, he joined Tara Arts to direct their first two professional productions, *Lion's Raj* and *Ancestral Voices.* A year later he was appointed Artistic Director of Contact Theatre in Manchester where his productions included, *Romeo and Juliet, A Midsummer Night's Dream, The Duchess of Malfi, Blood Wedding* (Manchester Evening News Best Production Award), *Mother Courage and her Children, Oedipus, To Kill A Mockingbird* (Manchester Evening News Best Production Award), *The Power of Darkness* and new plays *Two Wheeled Tricycle* by John Chambers, *Face Value* by Cindy Artiste, *Green* by Tony Clark, *Homeland* by Ken Blakeson and *McAlpine's Fusiliers* by Kevin Fegan. He joined Birmingham Repertory Theatre Company in 1990 as Associate Director. His many productions there include *Macbeth, Julius Caesar, The Atheist's Tragedy* (TMA Best Director Award), *The Seagull, Of Mice and Men, Threepenny Opera, Saturday Sunday Monday, The Grapes of Wrath, The Playboy of the Western World, Pygmalion, St Joan, The Entertainer* and David Lodge's *Home Truths.* In 1997 he was appointed Associate Artistic Director responsible for the launch and programme of The Door (formerly The Rep Studio), dedicated exclusively to the promotion of new work. His recent productions there include *Playing by The Rules* by Rod Dungate, *Nervous Women* by Sara Woods, *Rough* by Kate Dean, *Syme* (co-production with NT Studio) by Michael Bourdages, *True Brit* by Ken Blakeson, *Confidence* by Judy Upton, *Down Red Lane* by Kate Dean, *Paddy Irishmen* (co-production with the Tricycle Theatre) by Declan Croghan, *All That Trouble* by Paul Lucas, *Silence* (co-production with Theatre Royal Plymouth) by Moira Buffini, *My Best Friend* (co-production with Hampstead Theatre) by Tamsin Oglesby, *Slight Witch* (co-production with NT Studio) by Paul Lucas and *Belonging* by Kaite O'Reilly. He has freelanced extensively including *Dr Faustus* (The Young Vic), *The Red Balloon* (Bristol Old Vic and RNT – TMA Best Show for Young People Award), *The Snowman* (Leicester Haymarket), *Mother Courage and Her Children* (RNT), *The Day After Tomorrow* (RNT), *The Wood Demon* (Playhouse) and *Loveplay* (RSC) by Moira Buffini.

His writing credits include: *Hand it to Them* (Orange Tree 1982), *Gone Egon* (Riverside Studios 1983), *The Power of Darkness* (Orange Tree 1983). *Wake* (Orange Tree 1984), *Tide Mark* (RSC 1984), *Green* (Contact Theatre 1985), *Matter of Life and Death* (National Theatre). His adaptations for children which have been produced throughout the country include: *The Snowman, The Little Prince, The Red Balloon, Pinocchio* and *The Pied Piper*.

He has recently left The REP to pursue his writing and freelance directing interests: *Tender* by Abi Morgan (Hampstead Theatre & Tour); *The Red Balloon* (BBC Radio 4); *Winnie the Witch* (The Door, Birmingham Repertory Theatre).

Korky Paul
Illustrator

Korky Paul was born in Harare, Zimbabwe in 1951, into a family of seven children. His real name is Hamish Vigne Christie Paul. He enjoyed a wild and privileged childhood in the African Bushveldt. At an early age he was reading comic books and scribbling cartoons.

He scribbled his way through Durban School of Art and for four years scribbled at an advertising agency in Cape Town. In 1976, as Korky puts it, he 'fled for Europe' and landed up in Greece. Here he met a mad Scot, James Watt, working for a Greek publisher, who commissioned Korky to illustrate a series of educational books teaching Greek children to speak the 'Queen's English'. And so he began his career as a children's book illustrator.

He spent some time working in an advertising agency in London and Los Angeles, and then studied film animation under Jules Engel at CAL-ARTS, California. Korky's first children's book was a pop-up called *The Crocodile and the Dumper Truck* published in 1980, with paper engineering by Ray Marshall.

In 1986 Korky Paul met the editor Ron Heapy at Oxford University Press who commissioned him to illustrate *Winnie the Witch*. It won the Children's Book Award in 1987 and has been published in over 10 languages. Korky has since illustrated more very successful books for Oxford University Press, Random House, Penguin and many other publishers. Three of Korky's picture books have been adapted for CD-ROM: *Dragon Poems, Winnie the Witch* and *The Fish Who Could Wish,* which won the coveted European Multi-Media Award (EMMA) in 1995. Korky Paul has very quickly become a well-known figure in the children's book world and he is especially popular with the young children who read his books and are carried away into a fantasy world by the illustrations.

Valerie Thomas
Writer

Valerie Thomas was born in Australia and has lived there for most of her life, but she has also lived in England, France and Norway. She has travelled to most parts of the world, even Antarctica, and she is now trying to organise her life so that she never has to experience another winter. She used to live with a big black cat exactly like Wilbur, but luckily her house was not black.

Mark Vibrans
Composer

Training: Bretton Hall, Wakefield.
Mark has written scores for *Oedipus Rex, A Midsummer Night's Dream, Mother Courage, Blood Wedding, McAlpine's Fusilier, Dr Faustus, Dracula, Cinderella* and *Romeo and Juliet* (Contact Theatre); *Dr Faustus and Coriolanus* (Young Vic); *A Midsummer Night's Dream, A View From the Bridge, Romeo and Juliet, Love's Labour's Lost, Richard II* and *All's Well That Ends Well* (Manchester Royal Exchange*); Odysseus Thump* (West Yorkshire Playhouse); *Macbeth, Cider With Rosie, The Pied Piper, The Atheist's Tragedy, Peter Pan, A Doll's House, Pinocchio* and *Julius Caesar* (Birmingham Repertory Theatre); *Titus Andronicus, Possession* and *Macbeth* (Bolton Octagon); *B-Road Movie, Move Over Moriarty, King Arthur* and *Women on the Verger* (Lip Service); *The Day After Tomorrow, Mother Courage* and *The Red Balloon* (Royal National Theatre); *Pericles, Julius Caesar and Henry V* (RSC).
Mark's adaptations of *The Little Prince* and *The Red Balloon,* written with Anthony Clark, have been widely performed.

Rachel Blues
Designer

Rachel trained at Edinburgh College of Art and Bristol Old Vic Theatre School.
Recent designs include: *Top Girls* (BAC, Oxford Stage Company, West End and UK Tour 2002); *The Sleepers Den* (Southwark Playhouse); *Loveplay* (Royal Shakespeare Company: The Pit);

Ham (New Vic Theatre, Stoke); *Belonging, Silence* (Birmingham Repertory Theatre); *The Dove* (Warehouse Theatre Croydon); *Bouncers* (Octagon Theatre Bolton/Belgrade Theatre Coventry); *Car* (Theatre Absolute, Coventry Belgrade – winner of Fringe First); *Inmate Death* (Gate London). For the Coliseum Theatre, Oldham: *Rebecca, Brimstone and Treacle, Keeping Tom Nice, Lucky Sods, Second From Last in the Sack Race, Dead Funny, The Cemetery Club, Dancin' in the Street* and costumes for *Alfie – The Musical.* For the Swan Theatre Worcester, *Charley's Aunt, Private Lives* and *Elsie and Norm's Macbeth.*

Tim Mitchell
Lighting Designer

For Birmingham Repertory Theatre Company: *Of Mice and Men, Hamlet* and *Twelfth Night* (and national tour), *Absurd Person Singular, St Joan, My Best Friend* (and Hampstead Theatre); *Paddy Irishman, Paddy Englishman and Paddy...* (and Tricycle), *Frozen, Whisper of Angels' Wings, The Cherry Orchard , True Brit, Dr Jekyll and Mr Hyde, Romeo and Juliet, The Merchant of Venice, Macbeth, Old Times, Peter Pan* and *The Atheist's Tragedy* (Gold Medal winner at the 1995 Prague Quadrennial).

Other productions include: *Noises Off* (Royal National Theatre/ No.1 tour/Piccadilly Theatre/Broadway); *King John, Jubilee, The Lieutenant of Inishmore. Henry IV Parts I and II, Macbeth, Romeo and Juliet, The Winter's Tale, Oroonoko* (RSC); *Mahler's Conversion* (Aldwych Theatre); *Edward II* and *Mojo* (Crucible Sheffield); *Hamlet* (Elsinore, Denmark); *Ain't Misbehavin* (Derby Playhouse); *A Lie of the Mind* and *Merrily We Roll Along* (Donmar); *The Lady Vanishes* (Colchester Mercury/No.1); *A Small Family Business* (Chichester Theatre); *Speaking in Tongues* (Derby Playhouse, Hampstead Theatre); *Pyjama Game* (Toronto/New Victoria House Theatre); *Danny Bouncing* (Derby Playhouse); *A Raisin in the Sun* (Young Vic); *Two Pianos, Four Hands* (Comedy Theatre); *Dames at Sea* (Ambassadors Theatre); *The Red Balloon* and *The Alchemist* (RNT); *The Entertainer* (West Yorkshire Playhouse); *Our Boys* (Derby Playhouse/Donmar) and *The Snowman* (Peacock Theatre, London).

Opera and dance credits include: *The Marriage of Figaro, Don Giovanni, Requiem Ballet* (Kammeroper Vienna); *Yeoman Of The Guard* (D'Oyle Carte); *Carmen Negra* (Icelandic Opera); *On The Town* (London Symphony Orchestra/Barbican/BBC TV); *Prometheus* (Berlin Symphony Orchestra).

Future productions include: *High Society* and *Richard III*, with Kenneth Branagh (Crucible, Sheffield).

THE REP

Birmingham Repertory Theatre

Birmingham Repertory Theatre is one of Britain's leading national theatre companies. From its base in Birmingham, The REP produces over twenty new productions each year. Under the new Artistic Direction of Jonathan Church, The REP has enjoyed great success with one of its busiest and most exciting programmes ever.

The commissioning and production of new work lies at the core of The REP's programme. In 1998 the company launched The Door, a venue dedicated to the production and presentation of new work. This, together with an investment of almost £1 million over four years in commissioning new drama from some of Britain's brightest and best writing talent, gives The REP a unique position in British theatre. Indeed, through the extensive commissioning of new work The REP is providing vital opportunities for the young and emerging writing talent that will lead the way in the theatre of the future. This season we have enjoyed Abi Morgan's *Tender* and Gurpreet Kaur Bhatti's first play, *Behsharam* (*Shameless*), with next season including plays by Kaite O'Reilly, Moira Buffini, Lloyd Withers, Lisa Evans and visits from Paines Plough and Shared Experience.

REP productions regularly transfer to London and tour nationally and internationally. In the last 24 months many of our productions have been seen in London including *Two Pianos, Four Hands, Baby Doll, My Best Friend, Terracotta, The Gift, The Snowman, A Wedding Story, Out In The Open, Tender, Behsharam* and *The Ramayana* at The Royal National Theatre. Our production of *Hamlet* also played in repertoire with *Twelfth Night* on a major UK tour last year and in August played in the grounds of Elsinore Castle, Denmark as part of their annual Shakespeare Festival.

Developing new and particularly younger audiences is also at the heart of The REP's work. In its various Education initiatives, such as Transmissions, The Young REP, Page To Stage, as well as with the programming of work in The Door for children. The REP's Play Ups series are always in great demand and the perfect introduction to the excitement of live theatre for small children. This Christmas, we are delighted to bring the wonderful world of *Winnie The Witch* to life for just that age group and next June we present Philip Ridley's award-winning book *Krindlekrax* on the main stage for 9-15 years.

Theatre for the world. Made in Birmingham.

www.birmingham-rep.co.uk

Winnie the Witch first published 1987, *Winnie in Winter* first published 1996, *Winnie Flies Again* first published 1999, all by Oxford University Press.

This adaptation first published in 2001 by Oberon Books Ltd. (incorporating Absolute Classics)
521 Caledonian Road, London N7 9RH
Tel: 020 7607 3637 / Fax: 020 7607 3629
e-mail: oberon.books@btinternet.com

Winnie the Witch adapted for the stage by Anthony Clarke, based on *Winnie the Witch, Winnie in Winter* and *Winnie Flies Again*, by Korky Paul and Valerie Thomas © Oxford University Press 1987, 1996, 1999.

A catalogue record for this book is available from the British Library.

ISBN: 1 84002 255 8

Cover illustration: Korky Paul, reproduced from *Winnie the Witch* by Korky Paul and Valerie Thomas, by permission of Oxford University Press.

Printed in Great Britain by Antony Rowe Ltd, Reading.

Characters

People

WINNIE the WITCH

PILOTS and PASSENGERS

ICE CREAM SELLER

OPTICIAN

DEAD-EYED PAUL the PIRATE

CROWD

Puppets

WILBUR the CAT

CROC

SNAKE

SNOUT

STRIPE

COMB

BIRDS

FROGS

CREEPY CRAWLIES (SPIDERS and INSECTS)

CREATURES
who live under Winnie's bed, and in the
darker recesses of her house

FLOWERS

MOGG
Pirate Paul's ginger moggy

Company
This play can be performed by as few as five
actor/singer/musician/puppeteers. The puppets are to range
in size and type to best reveal the humour, magic,
poignancy of the story.

Design
The set, costumes and props should reflect, at all times,
the imagination, wit and ingenuity of Korky Paul's
original illustrations.

Music
The music cues in this text refer to the score for the first
production at Birmingham Rep, composed by Mark
Vibrans. This music is available for usage; enquiries
should be made through the author's agent.

List of Songs

Part One

1. Trouble
2. Trouble (reprise)
3. Wee Willy Wilbur
4. A Cat in a Million
5. Zoom Broom

Part Two

1. Zoom Broom (reprise)
2. Set Sail
3. Sea-Dog
4. Zoom Broom (reprise)
5. Song of Summer
6. A Cat in a Million (reprise)

PART ONE

Scene 1

WINNIE's black kitchen.

WILBUR, a black cat, asleep on a patchwork, black, quilted cushion balanced precariously on top of a large black upside-down cooking pot.

Music 1.

WINNIE: (*Off.*) Wilbur! Wilbur!

> *WILBUR opens his green eyes.*

Have you been playing with my sock?

WILBUR: I haven't touched your sock.

> *WILBUR goes back to sleep.*

> *WINNIE enters, dressed in her blue dress, custom-designed witch's hat, mauve housecoat, yellow ribbon in her hair and one sock/stocking. She props her damaged broomstick against the wall.*

WINNIE: With everything in this house turned black to hide the mess you'd think it'd be easy to find a red and yellow sock. Sock, sock wherever you are...

> *WINNIE searches a basket of twigs near the cauldron, carelessly, sending WILBUR flying across the room.*

I'm sorry, Wilbur, I didn't see you there.

> *WILBUR settles himself on WINNIE's chair as WINNIE continues to look for her sock.*

Where could it be? When did I last have it? When did I...? Last night! Last night I tripped over you Wilbur;

stubbed my toe; took my sock off to rub the bruise; noticed my nail was broken and hanging by a thin thread of skin… Where are the scissors I used to cut it – help me, Wilbur! You must've seen where I put my sock. They're my favourite socks.

WILBUR: They're your only pair.

WINNIE: The summer is nearly over. My feet are cold. I've got spells to prepare, magic to do, and a broomstick that needs mending if we're ever going to fly again. (*To the CREATURES who live in the darker recesses of the room.*) Have any of you creepy crawlies, been playing with my sock?

CROC appears out of the darkness.

Sock Croc?

CROC shakes his head.

Sock, sock wherever you are –

WINNIE picks up a pair of scissors and sits down on her chair.

Here are the scissors. My sock won't be far away –

WILBUR is squashed in the chair.

WILBUR: Aggh! You're hurting me!

WINNIE: Get out of it! It's your own fault Wilbur. If you didn't keep falling asleep, this wouldn't keep happening.

WILBUR: If you looked where you were going, this wouldn't keep happening. I'm a cat, Winnie. And cats like to sleep. We like to dream. In my dreams, Winnie, I'm in a much nicer place than here with you…sitting, and treading and falling over me the whole time.

WILBUR retreats to sleep on the floor, well out of WINNIE's path.

WINNIE: It's because you're as black as everything else in this house.

WILBUR: It's because you can't see properly. I was black before the house was.

WINNIE: If you slept with your eyes open I'd always know where you were.

WILBUR: That's impossible. (*Referring to sock.*) It's under the chair.

WINNIE: Fish do.

WILBUR: I'm not a fish.

WINNIE: You've got lovely green eyes Wilbur. They glisten like emeralds on a velvet cushion. Try sleeping with them open.

WILBUR: Who are you calling a cushion? Just because you keep sitting on me, doesn't mean I'm a cushion!

WINNIE: (*Changing the subject to comfort him.*) Purr for me Wilbur, purr…

WILBUR: I don't feel like it. Put your socks on.

WINNIE: You had no right to be sleeping on my bed last night. How many times have I said, 'I don't mind you having fleas, hiccoughing up your fur balls, and shedding your hair, anywhere in this house, but not on my bed!'? It irritates my sleep.

WILBUR: You irritate mine.

WINNIE: (*Ignoring WILBUR.*) Pah! I remember…

WINNIE finds her sock under the chair.

Ha! Ha!

Music 2.

She turns it the right way out and shakes a spider out of the toe. WILBUR jumps on the spider and toys with it, while WINNIE puts on her sock.

WINNIE, dressed to perfection, dances around the room with relief. WILBUR dives into a flat basket of twigs to escape her cavorting.

The dance comes to an end. WINNIE collapses in her chair. The music stops.

Oh Wilbur… Pass me my broomstick.

WILBUR ignores her. WINNIE fetches her damaged broomstick herself.

Look at the state of this. There was a time when the sky was empty and to jump on a broomstick was a wonderful way to travel. No traffic lights. No traffics jams. A time past. Now the sky is crowded with balloons, gliders, planes, para-gliders, rockets and kites all dodging each other and attacking me like bees the rose bush. The helicopter that shaved the brush off this could've had my hair… And my hair is my most attractive feature.

WILBUR: It's not attractive.

WINNIE: We were lucky to escape with our lives.

WILBUR: You should look where you're going.

WINNIE: It was my right of way.

WILBUR: It's always your right of way.

WINNIE: It's not me that can't see.

WINNIE lays the broomstick across her knees and starts to repair it, forcing twigs from the basket into the head.

WILBUR: Then how do you explain why you keep tripping over me?

WINNIE: We know why that is…

Music 3.

You're trouble Wilbur, big, big trouble!

'Trouble.'

We both agreed that to ease the stress,
Of living together in each other's mess
I'd magic our house black, and thus disguise
All our jumble and rubbish from prying eyes.
You'll agree it looks neater and the colour's a treat,
But the downside is you Wilbur, under my feet.

You're trouble Wilbur,
Big, big trouble.

WILBUR: It's not my fault that my colouring's black.
It's part of tradition like your broom and your hat,
Black's always been lucky for a witch's cat,
Until you started messing with my habitat.
Now everywhere I settle you squash me flat –
And keep on using me like an old doormat.

You're trouble Winnie,
Big, big trouble.

WINNIE: We've got no future as a well-knit team,
Unless I can manage to turn you green,
Green against black is beautifully clear
With your green eyes open you don't disappear,
Imagine it Wilbur, if you were all green,
You'd be no more trouble for you'd always be seen.

No trouble Wilbur,
No more trouble.

WILBUR: I'm camouflaged to match the walls,
The spiral stairs and the marble floors,
You could magic them back to the colour they were –

21

WINNIE: And tidy our mess, if you'd really prefer –
Oh Wilbur this broom wasn't made to sweep floors,
And you were not made to be tortured indoors.
Green is the colour of freedom and hope,
Green is the colour that'll give you the scope,
To be noticed and greeted wherever you roam,
Crossing roads, on my broom, at sea and at home
Green is the colour that'll help to restore.
The way that we were – best friends like before.

WINNIE sorts through her beaker of wands. Chooses her wand and flicks through her book of spells.

Let's be a brave witch and cat partnership,
I'll grab my wand –

WILBUR: – while I bite my lip.
Winnie assure me you've read the whole spell?
I'm feeling so nervous…

WINNIE: …but looking so well.
I'm very prepared with my wand at the ready,
Stop shivering Wilbur, be brave and stand steady!

Trouble Wilbur.
No more trouble.

Ready?

WINNIE raises her wand closes her eyes, her protruding purple lips start to twitch.

Abracadab –

WILBUR: Wait!

WINNIE freezes.

You won't turn me into a frog, will you? I've seen what you do to frogs…

WINNIE takes a frog out of her pocket and drops it into the saucepan on the stove.

WINNIE: I've invested a lot of time and cat food in you, and I've trusted you with some powerful, powerful secrets. I'm not going to change you into a frog and have to get myself a new kitten… I'm not going to train some ambitious little mog like Meg's with no respect for experience who thinks he can do it all…oh no… I've nurtured you Wilbur and I couldn't do my job without you. A witch without her familiar, her trusty black cat, her Wilbur…is like a house without a roof. Useless.

WILBUR: And tradition says I should be black, doesn't it?

WINNIE: Tradition says I should wear a black hat, but I don't. And it doesn't affect how good I am, does it? My granny had a black hat but I've cast more spells than she ever did. If you want to be a slave to tradition Wilbur, you can kiss the future goodbye. Are you ready?

WILBUR nods. WINNIE raises her wand, closes her eyes, her protruding purple lips start to twitch. Again.

Abracadabra!

WINNIE waves her wand.

Music 4.

The lights flicker. Darkness. Lights up. Nothing has happened.

Wrong wand.

WINNIE goes over to her collection and pulls out another wand. WILBUR shakes.

WILBUR: I'd like a saucer of milk.

WINNIE: Trust me.

WILBUR: I do, Winnie. And if I don't like being green, you will reverse the spell, won't you Winnie?

WINNIE prepares herself again.

You can, can't you Winnie? Winnie?

WINNIE: Ready?

WINNIE raises the wand, closes her eyes, and once more her protruding purple lips start to twitch. She describes a circle with the tip of the wand.

Abracadabra!

Music 5.

The house is filled with green light. As the music intensifies the green light contracts, until it is focused tightly on WILBUR, and WILBUR alone. A flash. A crash. Blackout.

Lights up. Sweet music as a green WILBUR stands in place of the black one.

Music 6.

WINNIE: How does that feel?

WILBUR: Green.

WINNIE: You can sleep where you like now Wilbur.

Music 7. 'Trouble' (Reprise).

WINNIE/CHORUS: You're my familiar witch's cat,
As dear to me as my pointed hat,
And now I've magicked your black coat green
There's nowhere in this house you can't be seen –
Be happy sweet Wilbur, for the colour really suits,
You're a one off green breed, you're ever so cute.

By waving my wand
No more trouble.

Give praise to my wand
No more trouble!

Scene 2

Music 8.

WINNIE's garden – more of a meadow than a green lawn. To one side, her uncultivated rose bush, and to the other a tall tree. In the distance centre WINNIE's backdoor, ajar.

SNAKE, CROC, SNOUT, STRIPE and COMB (in dark glasses) are lazing in the sun.

SNAKE: Croc? Croc?

SNOUT: What?

SNAKE: I wasn't talking to you Snout. I was talking to Croc. Keep your snout out of this.

WINNIE: (*From inside the house.*) Wilbur!

SNOUT: Croc, Snake's talking to you.

CROC: It's only when you get out you realise how cold the house is…

STRIPE: It's the colour. It's as dark and cold as a winter's night in there.

WINNIE: (*From inside the house.*) Wilbur, where are you?

COMB: Winter's on its way, but it's too early for Snake to hibernate.

SNOUT: Far too early.

COMB: It'd upset his rhythm.

SNOUT: You might never wake up.

SNAKE: Fancy a game of hide and seek, Croc?

CROC: No.

WINNIE: (*From inside the house. Sweetly.*) Wilbur, Wilbur, I've got something for you…

SNOUT: I'll play with you, Snake.

SNAKE: Anyone else? Comb?

WINNIE: (*Off.*) Wilbur! Get off!

COMB: Have you noticed how Wilbur's been putting on weight?

WINNIE: (*From inside the house.*) Get off my bed!

STRIPE: It stands to reason. Ever since he's been green the birds don't see him coming.

WINNIE: (*From inside the house.*) Off!

CROC: Feel the heat of that autumn sun!

SNAKE: Stripe, do you want to play?

WINNIE: (*From inside the house.*) If I've told you once, I've told you a thousand times, you're not to sleep on my bed.

STRIPE: Yesterday Wilbur ate four sparrows for breakfast, two magpies and a wood pigeon for lunch, a rare bird with red, white and blue feathers about half past three, a peacock for tea, and he left a chaff finch under Winnie's chair for a midnight feast.

CROC: I had that.

WINNIE: (*From inside the house.*) If you don't get off my bed you'll spend the whole day in the garden!

SNOUT: Here comes trouble.

STRIPE: When did he catch the parrot?

ALL: Parrot?

STRIPE: The red, white and blue one?

COMB: It wasn't a parrot.

SNOUT: It was a rare bird.

ALL: Well, it looked like a parrot.

SNAKE: Are you going to play, Stripe?

STRIPE: Only if I can hide first.

WINNIE: (*From inside the house.*) Off! By the time I count three!

SNAKE: I'm hiding first. It was my idea.

WINNIE: (*From inside the house.*) One!

SNAKE: You can hide next.

SNOUT: No he can't. The first one to find Snake is the next to hide.

COMB: You noticed, how Winnie's in a much better mood since she turned him green?

SNOUT: Not today she isn't.

STRIPE: It stands to reason, she isn't falling over him anymore. She was covered in bruises, with a temper on her like a bull. Turning Wilbur green was her revenge –

SNAKE: Gone wrong.

STRIPE: – for him getting under her feet the whole time.

SNOUT: But now he can't sleep on her black bed without being seen and he's unhappy.

WINNIE: (*From inside the house.*) Two!

CROC: I don't care how much pain she was in, she should never have taken it out on us.

ALL: (*Nodding.*) Hmmm!

CROC: We're always busy minding our own business.

COMB: Except for Snout.

CROC: It's in our nature. We're creepy-crawlies, good at keeping out of the way, except that day she was looking for her grandmother's book of spells.

SNOUT: It's her fault she couldn't find it what with everything being black.

ALL: We know.

CROC: She was in a terrible state, blaming everyone for losing it and we'd never seen the book before. And then she thought she remembered it was under the bed, our favourite hiding place, in her treasure chest with all the rest of her secrets.

WINNIE: (*Off.*) Wilbur!

CROC: And while we were mid-morning snacking on daddy long legs, she scared us stupid by dragging the chest out... I mean, she hadn't moved it in years, had she? And then when she couldn't find the book, she slammed the top down, and pushed back the chest with such force that I lost a claw. Well, I nearly did.

SNOUT: Three!

STRIPE: It was I who lost my tail.

CROC: And it took you two hours to grow a new one.

WINNIE: (*From inside the house.*) Two and a half!

SNAKE: (*Slithering away into the undergrowth.*) Well, I'm off to hide!

CROC/STRIPE/COMB: We're not playing!

WINNIE: (*From inside the house.*) Two and three quarters!

SNOUT: I'll count to a hundred, Snake. Will that give you time?

SNAKE: Eyes closed. I know what you're like Snout, you'd cheat on your best friend.

CROC: He hasn't got a best friend.

WINNIE: (*From inside the house.*) Two and three quarters and a little bit more!

COMB: We provide the ingredients for Winnie's magic. Without our venom, spit and tears, scales, nails and limbs she couldn't concoct a potion to save an ant. It's thanks to us she can have herself a good time, heal people, make liars tell the truth, and thieves give back what they have stolen.

WINNIE: (*From inside the house.*) Three!

CROC/STRIPE/COMB: Trouble!

SNOUT: Four!

SNAKE: (*From somewhere in the undergrowth.*) Don't cheat Snout! You start with one, and you count slowly...very slowly.

SNOUT counts to a hundred through the rest of the scene.

WINNIE opens the back door, shakes the contents out of her black checked quilt – a fat green WILBUR.

WINNIE: *Pah!* And don't think you're coming back in until you promise me you'll never, ever, ever do that again.

WINNIE goes back into the house. WILBUR waddles through the grass.

SNOUT: (*To WILBUR.*) Do you want to play hide and seek?

STRIPE: If you let Wilbur play, no one will ever find him. We don't stand a chance in this grass.

Music 9.

WILBUR settles down in the grass. A BIRD circles the area...hovers.

CROC: (*To the BIRD.*) I wouldn't be feeding here, rare bird. Not if I were you...

The BIRD settles in the grass. WILBUR pounces. A shower of blue, red and white feathers. WILBUR devours the BIRD.

The door opens and WINNIE appears with a letter.

WINNIE: Wilbur, be a good cat and read this letter for me. The handwriting's so small and as messy as a slug's trail. Please, Wilbur... I'll let you back in the house...

WILBUR: Only if I can lie on your bed!

WINNIE: No.

WILBUR: Tough.

WINNIE: You can't blackmail me.

The sound of SNOUT counting.

(*To CROC, SNOUT, STRIPE and COMB.*) Where is the little wretch? Can you see him?

SNOUT: Sorry, can't open my eyes.

COMB: He's over there somewhere. (*Pointing.*) See those feathers. Stupid bird.

WINNIE: (*Making her way towards the feathers.*) Wilbur you've got to read this for me. (*Trying to entice him to move.*) It's important. I think it's someone wanting to wish you an early *happy birthday.* Wilbur, Wilbur wherever you are...

WINNIE trips over WILBUR, somersaults three times into the rose bush. The letter goes flying, and her wand falls out of her pocket.

Aghhh!

CROC, STRIPE and COMB laugh. WINNIE doesn't appear to move. They go quiet.

SNOUT: Ninety-nine, one hundred! Ready or not, Snake, here I come!

WINNIE emerges from the rose bush tousled and furious.

Music 10.

WINNIE grabs her wand.

WINNIE: (*Waving it once.*) Abaracadabra!

The area fills with purple light. WILBUR rushes behind the rose bush for protection.

(*Waving her wand again.*) Abracadabra!

The area fills with red light.

(*Waving her wand again.*) Abracadabra!

The area fills with yellow light.

WILBUR: (*From behind the bush, whines.*) Miaow!

WINNIE: (*Waving her wand again.*) Abracadabra!

The area fills with pink light.

(*Waving her wand again.*) Abracadabra!

The area fills with blue light.

Come out from behind that bush and read me this letter!

WILBUR emerges from behind the rose bush, sheepishly. He has a red head, a yellow body, a pink tail, blue whiskers and four purple legs. CROC, STRIPE and COMB laugh at him.

Silence. WILBUR looks down at his legs. CROC, STRIPE and COMB laugh louder.

Silence. WILBUR looks at his tail. CROC, STRIPE and COMB laugh louder still.

Silence. WILBUR looks at his back and stomach. CROC, STRIPE and COMB laugh even louder.

WINNIE: That's better, now I'll be able to see you wherever you are.

WILBUR: What colour's my face?

COMB: Guess.

STRIPE: The same colour as the tip of Winnie's nose.

WILBUR: Red?

CROC: As the setting sun.

WILBUR: Whiskers?

WINNIE: Blue.

WILBUR: Blue…

COMB: As a summer sky.

All laugh.

WINNIE: This arrived this morning from Australia.

WILBUR: We don't know anyone in Australia.

WILBUR walks away disconsolate.

WINNIE: Wilbur… Wilbur, don't be upset. It's for your own good –

WILBUR climbs the tree.

WILBUR: Yours you mean.

WINNIE: Wilbur, come on. Come here. Don't sulk. You look ugly when you sulk.

WILBUR: I look ugly anyway. I suppose you think its funny when people stare at me as if there's something wrong with me…as if I'm not real! There's nothing wrong with me except I look like a parrot, and I'm supposed to be a cat!

WINNIE: You embrace your new colour Wilbur, and others will soon get used to you. Mark my words Wilbur, in a matter of days every cat will be wishing they were multicoloured.

All laugh.

(*To everyone.*) That'll do! You're not helping the situation. Wilbur come down out of that tree before I lose my temper!

WILBUR: You've lost it, already.

WINNIE: I can lose it again!

SNOUT reappears.

SNOUT: Snake's disappeared. I can't find him anywhere.

COMB, CROC and STRIPE point out WILBUR. SNOUT starts to laugh. WILBUR points.

WILBUR: He's in the pond.

SNOUT: (*Rushing off.*) Thank you Mr Lollipop.

ALL: (*Jeering.*) Lollipop, lollipop... Mr, Mr Lollipop!

CROC, STRIPE and COMB hurry off ahead of SNOUT.

COMB: First one there is the next one to hide.

SNOUT: You said you weren't playing.

STRIPE: Are *you* playing, Wilbur?

WINNIE: Wilbur, come down here and read me this letter for me or you don't come flying for a week. A whole week, do you hear? Well if you won't read this letter for me, I'm going in...I'm going in to... (*Holding back the tears.*) ...to find the biggest plasters I've got to cover the

33

injuries I've sustained falling into that bush… These cuts are stinging and bleeding like fountains.

SNOUT: Are they really?

STRIPE: Of course not. She wants him to feel sorry for her, that's all.

WINNIE: Tripping me up like that was unforgiveable. You'd have thought you'd have learnt your lesson when you were black. It really hurt… And I'm locking the door and jamming the cat flap.

WINNIE goes back into house. Time passes. The creatures leave to look for SNAKE. A variety of birds surround the tree.

Music 11. 'Wee Willy Wilbur.'

BIRDS: Wee Willy Wilbur
Wilbur's fur is
Red and yellow and blue
Winnie's cat has changed his strip
And we're not scared of you.
You know you look ridiculous –

WILBUR: Don't mock me I'm a cat

BIRDS: Dressed up like a stupid clown

WILBUR: I'm Wilbur. You know that!

BIRDS: Now we'll always see you coming
And escape your needle claws
No more birds for tea, poor Wilbur
No more feathers in your jaws.
Wee Willy Wilbur
Wilbur's fur is
Red and yellow and blue
Winnie's cat has changed his strip
And we're not scared of you.

Not a Burmese, Siamese Shorthair
Not a Russian Pixie Bob,
But a striped-lolly-Wilbur-wire-hair
That climbs up trees and sobs.

WILBUR: You know I feel an alien, the odd cat out that's me
Hungry, tired and ridiculed, stuck up in this tree,
All I want's my colour back, my old identity,
Oh Winnie come outside again, come out and rescue me!

BIRDS: Wee Willy Wilbur
Wilbur's fur is
Red and yellow and blue
Winnie's cat has changed his strip
And we're not scared of you.

WINNIE arrives.

WINNIE: Wilbur this is all your fault. It's late get down
from there!

WILBUR: Until you change my colour I'm not coming
anywhere.
Listen to their teasing Winnie, and if you really care
Please use your magic powers to return my sleek black
hair!

BIRDS: Wee Willy Wilbur
Wilbur's fur is
Red and yellow and blue
Winnie's cat has changed his strip
And we're not scared of you.

WINNIE comes back into the garden.

WINNIE: Wilbur, you stupid cat, it's late get down from
there!

WILBUR: Until you change my colour I'm not going
anywhere.
All the birds are teasing me, exacting their revenge,
And the moon's mocking smile is sending me deranged.

WINNIE: I hate to see you miserable. You know that I'm
your chum
But what else could I do, after all that you had done?
You have to face the facts Wil, life's very rarely fair,
But I'll forgive and then forget, if you climb down from
there.

Silence.

WILBUR: No.

WINNIE: Wilbur? Please… I don't like to see you miserable.

Silence.

BIRDS: Then Winnie had an idea.

Music 12.

*WINNIE waves her wand again and again and again and
again. The light changes colour accordingly. Blackout.*

Daylight. A black WILBUR in the tree. The birds fly away.

WINNIE: Now Wilbur, feeling better? It's time to read me
this letter.

WILBUR doesn't move.

The CREATURES return, lead by SNAKE.

What's the matter now?

WILBUR: The house is still black… What's the point of
coming in if you're going to tread on me, trip over my
back, and shout at me again?

WINNIE: Wilbur…

CREATURES: Winnie had another idea.

Music 13.

WINNIE waves her wand five times. The lights and music complement her action. Each stroke of the wand is punctuated with an Abracadabra!

Blackout.

A black WILBUR climbs down the tree.

Return to the Kitchen of Scene 1. All black has been charmed away. A full-colour interior.

Music 14. 'A Cat in a Million.'

WINNIE: That's better, more like it, you must be your
                                                    own cat,
I'm sorry for changing your colour like that
Though the mess in this house is still an issue
We'll have to clear it ourselves if magic won't do.

WILBUR sulks. WINNIE corrects herself.

(*Spoken.*) I will…

(*Sung.*) You're a cat in a million, you're sleek cool and wise,
With your elegant fur and your emerald green eyes,
Oh, what must I do to make you realise
Every moment I'm with you, life's a surprise.

I'll pick up my clothes, throw away the old food
I'll wash up the plates, pots and pans that we've used,
I'll puff up your cushion and make my brass bed,
Put the books on the shelves, put the tools in the shed.

CHORUS: He's a cat in a million, he's sleek cool and wise,
With his elegant fur and his emerald green eyes,
Oh, what must she do to make him realise
Every moment she's with him, life's a surprise.

WINNIE: You're a cat of distinction, my right hand man,
Whose always been there to help with my plans,
We must never be parted or row anymore,
Let's make up and shake on it, give me your paw.

They shake on it.

CHORUS: He's a cat in a million, he's sleek cool and wise,
    With his elegant fur and his emerald green eyes,
    Oh, what must she do to make him realise
    Every moment she's with him, life's a surprise.

WINNIE: Now I've magicked you back and you're feeling
                               much better
    You'll do me a favour and read me this letter…
    Oh where have I put it, oh why can't I cope?
    It's a bluish red-stripey air envelope.

CHORUS: He's a cat in a million, he's sleek cool and wise,
    With his elegant fur and his emerald green eyes,
    He had only to look and he easily spied,
    The letter that Winnie placed so nearby.

WILBUR finds the letter immediately.

WINNIE: Oh Wilbur you've found it, you brilliant black cat
    I'd have never been able to find things like that
    You're a cat of distinction, you're my right hand man
    Come read me the letter and let's make a plan!

CHORUS: He's a cat in a million, he's sleek cool and wise,
    With his elegant fur and his emerald green eyes,
    Oh, what must she do to make him realise
    Every moment she's with him, life's a surprise.

WINNIE: Whose it from? What does it say?

WILBUR: (*Scanning the letter.*) It's from a Mr… Dead-eyed
    Pirate Paul… He says he's a well-known retired-pirate
    and artist, painting, currently, a series of pictures of well
    known witches.

WINNIE: Oh yes…

WILBUR: He's heard about you and would like to do a
    portrait…

WINNIE: You look surprised?

WILBUR: ...of me.

WINNIE: Of you? That is surprising. Are you sure?

WILBUR: You and me, together.

WINNIE: When?

WILBUR: As soon as he can.

WINNIE: Where?

WILBUR: In his Studio. Number 12, Lilac Avenue. Perth, Australia. He's got a cat called Mogg who wants to meet me.

WINNIE: We'd better get going then.

WILBUR: But this house is full of pictures of you. We don't need another one.

WINNIE: There's always room for one more. It's lucky I repaired the broomstick.

WILBUR: But do we have to fly? You know what happened the last time –

WINNIE: How else are we supposed to get there? Australia's on the other side of the world.

WILBUR: But –

WINNIE: We'll be more careful. You read the map, and I'll point the stick.

Music 15.

WINNIE presents a fully repaired broomstick, complete with stirrups, headlights and saddle. They mount.

Are you ready Wilbur? Hold on tight!

The music rises.

'Zoom Broom.'

WINNIE/WILBUR: Zoom broom zoom,
Zoom zimee zoom,
Zoom broom zoom,
Zimee zoom broom ZOOM!

The broom takes off. Blackout.

End of Part One.

PART TWO

Scene 1

Music 16.

Lights up on WINNIE and WILBUR on their broomstick, flying over cities and countryside, forests, reservoirs and crowded motorways. There is a globe mounted on the boomstick. WILBUR is attempting to navigate. A broken red line describes their flight path.

'Zoom Broom.'

WILBUR/WINNIE: Zoom broom, zoom!
   Zoom, zimee zoom,
   Zoom broom, zoom!
   Zimee zoom broom zoom.

A busy sky: a balloonist, a bi-plane, a jumbo jet, a rocket, a helicopter. WINNIE gets in their way causing chaos and 'air rage'.

WILBUR: Take your first left leaving England,
   Then turn right through rural France,
   Loop the loop to the heel of Italy,
   Crossing the blue Adriatic Sea.

WINNIE whips her broomstick with her wand.

WILBUR/WINNIE: Zoom broom, zoom!
   Zoom, zimee zoom,
   Zoom broom, zoom!
   Zimee zoom broom zoom.

WILBUR: Right for Greece and Saudi Arabia,
   Fly the length of the thin Red Sea,
   Left for India and Malaysia,
   Straight on to Perth Australia.

WILBUR/WINNIE: Zoom broom, zoom!
    Zoom, zimee zoom,
    Zoom broom, zoom!
    Zimee zoom broom zoom.

WILBUR: Winnie take care!
    See that balloon over there!
    There's a bi-plane that seems to have strayed.
    A jumbo full of people,
    A rocket and a steeple!
    And all of them heading this way!

Shouts of indignation from irate PILOTS and PASSENGERS.

WILBUR/WINNIE: Zoom broom, zoom!
    Zoom, zimee zoom,
    Zoom broom, zoom!
    Zimee zoom broom zoom.

WILBUR: Dive duck and soar,
    High above the uproar,
    Of the 'air rage' you seem to have caused.
    For the sake of a picture,
    I'm losing my whiskers,
    My tail's been stretched, crimped and shorn!

PILOTS/PASSENGERS: Winnie take care!
    You're not safe in the air!
    Your stunts on that broom, don't impress!
    Find your own air lane
    Away from our planes
    Before you cause someone to crash!

WILBUR: Winnie take care!
    Or we'll never get there!
    Face front and look where we're going!
    A hang glider tower
    Very tall mountain
    Is going to get in your way.

ALL: Zoom broom, zoom!
   Zoom, zimee zoom,
   Zoom broom, zoom!
   Zimee zoom broom zoom.

The broom stick crashes into the mountain, and free-falls to the ground. WINNIE looks much the worse for wear.

WINNIE: Do I look as bad as I feel?

WILBUR: Worse. You've got a bruise on your face the size of a beetroot, and a cut like a pirate's scar.

WINNIE: We'll never get there on this broomstick. The sky is too dangerous, Wilbur. There's people up there that want to do for me. We'll have to try something else.

WINNIE searches for her wand. She finds it. Waves it.

Abracadabra!

A bicycle is revealed in a puff of smoke.

Music 17.

WINNIE hangs her broomstick on it. Mounts. WILBUR hops on the back. WINNIE is extremely unsteady as she sets off…

WILBUR: Careful!

WINNIE: Don't worry, Wilbur. Once you know how to ride a bike, it's something you never forget. Like walking… And flying…if you're a witch.

WINNIE falls.

Wilbur, that was your fault. If you can't keep still how am I supposed to balance? Riding a bike is about balance, Wilbur. Balance and body strength.

WILBUR: I *was* being still.

WINNIE gets the hang of it again, and very slowly cycles off…

Music 18.

WINNIE: That's better. Hold on tight.

…off stage. While a stone and leafless tree are set in the playing area. WINNIE and WILBUR are heard off. A small bird in Uzbekistani national dress twitters on the branch of the tree.

(*Off.*) Where are we?

WILBUR: (*Off.*) Uzbekistan.

WINNIE: (*Off.*) Is it mountains all the way?

WILBUR: (*Off.*) Looks like it…all the way to India…

WINNIE and WILBUR ride on again, breathless. She's removed her socks. The bike wiggles.

WINNIE: Hello bird. We're looking for India.

The bird chirps and points.

It'll be winter by the time we get there.

WILBUR: Summer in Australia and winter in England.

WINNIE: This bike is so hard to pedal –

WILBUR: And so slow.

WINNIE: My muscles feel like jelly.

WILBUR: That's because you're not fit. Keep an eye out for the Khyber Pass. According to the map, it's a short cut to India. Hey Winnie, look at that!

Music 19.

WINNIE nearly crashes the bike as she swerves towards the tree, then the stone, then back to the tree, then off…

(*Going off.*) Watch out! Winnie, look where you're going! Stone! Tree! Tree! Stone! Help!

The music accelerates as WINNIE and WILBUR swerve off stage.

The tree and stone are replaced by a pond with frogs in it. The bike swerves back on, out of control, and crashes into the pond. Distressed flapping goldfish lie on the bank.

The music changes. (Lazy Frog Chorus: slow percussive.)

Music 20.

FIRST FROG: She should look where she's going, (*Croaks.*) she should.

SECOND FROG: Look – (*Croaks.*)

FIRST FROG: – where she is going, she should.

BOTH FROGS: Look! (*They croak together, twice.*)

WINNIE: Why did that pond have to get in the way?

WILBUR: I don't know Winnie, why did the balloon, the plane, the rocket, the stone the tree, the mountain, Me! Why does everything have to get in your way?

WINNIE: (*Retrieving her broomstick from the pond.*) Don't bear grudges Wilbur, whatever happened it's over now. A bicycle is worse than a broomstick Wilbur. We'll have to try something else.

The frogs jump on the handle bars of the bicycle and rides off.

Something fast!

(*Waving her wand.*) Abracadabra!

Music 21.

A large skateboard (more of a custom-made surf board with wheels) shoots on as the pond disappears. Hitching the broomstick to the underneath they set off at an incredible speed through South East Asia towards the Timor Sea/Indian Ocean.

Music 22.

This is so fast.

WILBUR: And so hard to steer.

WINNIE/WILBUR: And impossible to stop!

The countries shoot past, like cars on the motorway.

WINNIE: Indiaaaaaa!

WILBUR: Burmaaa!

WINNIE: Thailandand – and – and – and –

TOGETHER: Malaysia!

WILBUR: Indonesiaaaaaa!

WINNIE: Timor!

An ICE CREAM SELLER appears.

WINNIE/WILBUR: The Sea!

WINNIE and WILBUR crash into the ICE CREAM SELLER, scattering cornets and tubs everywhere.

ICE CREAM SELLER: Can't you see where you're going?

WINNIE: Not when you're in the way.

WILBUR: The Timor Sea. The tide's in our favour; the wind's in the right direction, we must set sail for Australia immediately.

ICE CREAM SELLER: What about the mess? How will you pay for all this?

WINNIE: When we get back. Don't worry, shan't forget. Promise. We'll help you when we get back.

ICE CREAM SELLER: (*Disgusted.*) Chaa!

Music 23. (Describing the sea.)

WILBUR: Once we're out to sea we bear left down the West Coast of Australia to Perth.

WILBUR and WINNIE retrieve their skateboard. They place the broomstick into a hole in the centre of the board and make a mast. WINNIE takes off her jacket and makes a sail. Waves her wand and produces a small rubber ring out of the inside of her hat to give to WILBUR. He inflates it.

They set sail.

'Set Sail.'

ALL: With the wind in your sails
Set sail, set sail, set sail, set sail
Ride the waves of the deep murky sea.

WINNIE waves to a distraught ICE CREAM SELLER.

Don't shed tears for the land
Or the friends that you're leaving
They'll never be far from your heart.
The sun is above
To guide, to guide, to guide your sails
And at night let the stars lead the way

Night falls. The sky is full of stars.

The moon is out laughing,
It knows you can't wait
For the morning to bring a new day.
Set sail, set sail, set sail, set sail
There's a new life for you on the way!

Day breaks. The sound of gulls.

WILBUR: Land ahoy! Land ahoy!

WINNIE: Where? Where, Wilbur? I can't see anything.

WILBUR: Now you tell me.

WINNIE: Oh yes, I can hear the gulls.

They arrive ashore. WILBUR jumps off the board first. Consults the globe and the sky.

WILBUR: Here we are then. This is Australia…

WINNIE: This is a beach.

WILBUR: And Perth is over there.

Collapsing the skateboard WINNIE notices the wheels.

WINNIE: These wheels are rusty. It's had it. We'll have to try something else. How about a hovercraft.

WILBUR: Don't bother it's not far. And besides we could do with the exercise. Look at those people! Aren't they beautiful.

WINNIE: Lying out like biscuits on a tray. Sunning parts of their bodies only the night should see. You wouldn't catch me wearing one of those. It's so hot here. I'm looking forward to getting back for winter. Aren't you Wilbur? Peace without all those creepy crawlies in the house. You still got Pirate Paul's address? Lead the way!

Music 24.

WILBUR starts off towards the audience, WINNIE in the opposite direction.

WILBUR: This way!

As they walk the sounds of people and busy street life increases. Enter two people carrying a log. They cross WINNIE's path. WILBUR walks under the log. WINNIE smacks straight into it. She is bent over it and carried off. The noise of the crowd is still getting louder. WILBUR continues for a few steps before realising that WINNIE isn't there. WILBUR panics.

Music 25.

(*In amongst the crowd, or even asking the audience.*) Excuse me have you seen Winnie? – Winnie the Witch? – Winnie! – Have you?

WINNIE enters still hanging off the log. (There may well be cries from the audience of 'She's behind you' 'Over there' etc.) By the time WILBUR realises was happening she's gone.

WILBUR leaves as WINNIE comes back. She is unceremoniously dumped on the ground. She attempts to get up and is hit three times by the log. The two carriers go off.

WINNIE gets up dazed and bruised.

WINNIE: Wilbur, I think I need a cup of tea. I'll go into this shop and order one. And a saucer of milk for you, no doubt? No doubt. Are you there, Wilbur?

Music 26. 'Cyclops' Optician's shop is established around WINNIE.

Scene 2

The Optician's shop. Racks of glasses and letter cards etc. In the background an OPTICIAN fitting a pair of glasses with a lens blacked out to a PIRATE with a patch. A ginger MOGGY in glasses, also with an eye patch, looks on.

OPTICIAN: Good day madam, can I help?

WINNIE: A cup of tea and a muffin please. And a saucer of milk for my tired cat.

OPTICIAN: I'm afraid, we don't sell cups of tea or muffins. But I think I can help you. Read this.

Enter WILBUR, as the OPTICIAN produces a letter card. She walks back twenty pigeon-paces and places WINNIE directly opposite it.

WILBUR: Winnie what are you doing in here? I've been half way around Perth looking for you?

WINNIE: Perth must be a very small place then.

OPTICIAN: Now Madam, could you read the top line for me?

WINNIE: Wilbur, this kind woman's going to help me.

WINNIE and MOGG eye each other up and down.

WILBUR: If you listen to her. I found out where Lilac Avenue is by the way. Hello. I'm Wilbur.

MOGG: Mogg.

OPTICIAN: Read.

WINNIE: (*Reading.*) I.

OPTICIAN: Good. Next line.

WINNIE: L. O.

OPTICIAN: Excellent.

WILBUR: (*To MOGG.*) My name's Wilbur. What's yours?

OPTICIAN: (*To WINNIE.*) Third line.

WINNIE: V. E. P. I. R.

OPTICIAN: Fourth line.

WILBUR: Are you blind in one eye?

MOGG: What's it to you?

WILBUR: Are you a pirate's cat?

WINNIE: H?

OPTICIAN: Continue…

WINNIE: T. B. – It's so difficult.

OPTICIAN: (*Placing a pair of glasses on WINNIE.*) Here, try these.

WILBUR: Is your name really Mogg? Do you know Dead-eyed Pirate Paul?

MOGG: (*Gasps.*) Dead-eyed Paul?

WINNIE: A. T. E. P. A. U. L. T. H. E. F. A. M. O. U. S. A. R. T. I. S. T

OPTICIAN: You're short-sighted.

WINNIE: I don't think so.

OPTICIAN: Try these. (*Placing another pair of glasses on WINNIE and handing her some text to read.*) Try reading off the card and board.

WINNIE: (*Nodding like a duck.*) I. L. O. V. E. P. I. R. A. T. E. P. A. U. L. T. H. E. F. A. M. O. U. S. A. R. T. I. S. T. I love Pirate Paul the famous artist.

PIRATE PAUL emerges from the back of the shop. Big hat, peg leg, eye patch.

PAUL: Yo, ho, ho who are you?

WINNIE and PAUL stare at each other. There's something there…

Hey, it's Winnie isn't it? Look Mogg, it's Winnie. Winnie the Witch from England. Of all the opticians in all the world this witch should walk into Cyclops. I dreamt I'd meet you today. It's you, isn't it? You, sitting here having your eyes tested in the Cyclops and me having my eye tested too. It's a rum-do. (*Doing a little jig with his peg leg.*) Do-da-di-do-da-di- day!

WINNIE: Who *are* you?

PAUL: You got my letter then?

WILBUR: That's why we're in Australia.

WINNIE: You mean, you're –

Music 27. 'Sea-Dog.'

PAUL: Mad sea-dog Pirate, Captain Paul
The most fearsome sea-dog of them all
Who put down the cutlass and the poisoned sword
Turned his back on the treasure, booty rich rewards,
The rum, the wenches and the screaming hoards
Of terrified opponents.
Sea-dog.

Instrumental as WINNIE looks on and PAUL flirtatiously sets up his painting materials. WILBUR and MOGG are getting it together as well...

WILBUR: I see you
You see me
Together we
Might, might be
Friends –
Friends forever?

MOGG: We'll see...

PAUL: Mad sea-dog pirate Captain Paul
The most fearsome sea-dog of them all
Who listened to his soul and answered its call
Turned from killing his foes to portrait painting
Bought a pencil and a brush from a stationery stall
Became a famous artist.
Sea-dog.

WILBUR: I like fish –

MOGG: So do I.

WILBUR: Together we –
Might might eat
Fish?
Fish together.

MOGG: We'll see.

WINNIE: Winnie the Witch, pleased to meet you Paul
  I'm the loveliest, kindest witch of all,
  This is my cat Wilbur, Wilbur please meet Paul,
  How should we pose, should we stand sit or sprawl?
  You can place us where you like, you're the expert Paul
  But I can't stay still for long.
  Sea-dog.

MOGG: I like sleep –

WILBUR: So do I.
  Together we –
  Might, might dream
  Dream together.

MOGG: We'll see.

PAUL: Your life's in your face, your soul's in your eyes,
  I can tell you're lost and lonely, looking for a guide
  I'm man of the world, the sort you'll rarely find,
  Rough and distinguished, threatening and kind.
  The perfect witch's mate.
  Sea-dog.

  *PAUL hands WINNIE the complete picture. WINNIE stares
  at it while the cats sing.*

MOGG: I like you –

WILBUR: You like me.
  Together we
  Will, will be

MOGG: Friends.

WILBUR: Friends forever?

MOGG: We'll see.

WINNIE: Is this really how you see me Paul?

It's not how I see myself at all.
Is my nose that big, are my ears that small?
Do my eyes bulge white like a pair of golf balls?
Those aren't my hands, I'm not a chinless turkey neck
My skin isn't splotchy and flecked.
Rude dog!

You can keep your picture, that isn't of me!
Back at home I'm a catch, and a real beauty,
Come on little Wilbur please give me your paw
There's nothing in Australia worth waiting for
I'll fly back with my glasses on, just you wait and see
How we dodge the traffic and trees
Let's fly!

WILBUR: (*To MOGG.*) It looks like I have to go.

MOGG: See ya!

WILBUR: I'll write if you write to me.

> *WINNIE and WILBUR mount the broomstick.*

PAUL: (*Starting another picture.*) I could always do another one.

> *Music 29. 'Zoom Broom' (Reprise).*

WILBUR/WINNIE: Zoom broom, zoom!
Zoom, zimee zoom,
Zoom broom, zoom!
Zimee zoom, broom zoom.

> *The sky fills with passing traffic.*

WINNIE: Wilbur, hooray!
We're up and away!
This time I can see where we're going!
I'll take the safe route
Dodging all in pursuit,
And be home by end of the day!

WILBUR/WINNIE: Zoom broom, zoom!
    Zoom, zimee zoom,
    Zoom broom, zoom!
    Zimee zoom, broom zoom.

PILOTS/PASSENGERS: Hey is that Winnie?
    That's Winnie, okay!
    Then why aren't we all in her way?
    She's got a new pair of glasses!
    This time she's learned her lesson
    Not to play bump in the skies.

    It's a miracle to me,
    Seems the blind witch sees
    That there's plenty of room for us all
    Hey Winnie, new eyes!
    Hey Winnie, surprise!
    Hey Winnie, you're Queen of the Skies.

    WINNIE and WILBUR fly home avoiding all obstacles.

WILBUR/WINNIE: Zoom broom, zoom!
    Zoom, zimee zoom,
    Zoom broom, zoom!
    Zimee zoom, broom zoom.

    It starts to snow.

    Music 30.

Scene 3

WINNIE's garden. Objects covered in white sheets representing mounds of snow and a thick white floor cloth. A window in the distance (two locations in one space) through which can be seen a Christmas tree and decorations (paper chain) being made. It's still snowing. CROC, STRIPE, SNOUT and COMB dressed in winter garb have just made themselves a snowman. It bears an uncanny resemblance to PIRATE PAUL... They shiver in the cold.

Outside.

COMB: Who does it remind you of? Guess!

SNOUT: Peter Pan.

COMB: Are you stupid?

ALL: He is.

COMB: Peter Pan wasn't a pirate.

STRIPE: Captain Hook?

CROC: (*Of the snowman.*) Mad sea-dog Dead-eyed Paul!

COMB: (*Sings.*) Sea-dog!

SNOUT: Hey, guess what?

ALL: What?

SNOUT: The fountain's frozen.

ALL: So?

SNOUT: So.

ALL: So we all saw that.

SNOUT: And did you see the frog that's frozen mid jump –

STRIPE: It's little legs sticking out of the ice, like a tele ariel... yeh, yeh we seen it.

SNOUT: I thought you might not have, that's all.

ALL: Well we have.

CROC: Make a nice couple of frog flavoured ice-pops for Wilbur.

STRIPE: If only it was summer...

ALL: If only.

COMB: I can't seem to hibernate this year and I really need to.

ALL: Don't we all.

COMB: Still Snake's managed it.

SNOUT: I bet you Winnie doesn't like our snowman. I bet you she turns him into a –

Inside.

Music 31.

Enter WILBUR through a cat flap (perhaps).

WINNIE: (*Hanging a paper chain on the tree.*) Wilbur, help me.

WILBUR: Just let me th-th-th-thaw my paws, and m-m-m-melt the ice off of-of-of my whiskers.

WINNIE: (*Making a paper chain.*) Have you ever wondered Wilbur why it is when you're young you're always looking forward to winter by the end of summer and summer by the end of winter? Why it is, once you've lived through a few long winters, you dread the winter? Two weeks of winter is plenty for me.

WILBUR: What do you want for Christmas, Winnie?

WINNIE: Summer.

WILBUR: Do you know what I want?

WINNIE: I do. I really do. Pass me my spell book.

WILBUR: Guess!

WINNIE: Summer?

WILBUR: And?

WINNIE: Summer, Wilbur. Imagine if we could only have a little patch of summer in the middle of winter, I'd smile all day long…

WILBUR: There's plenty of summer in Australia right now.

WINNIE: We're not going back. Imagine… Oh Wilbur, I hate to see you miserable, have you heard from Mogg recently?

WILBUR: You know I haven't.

WINNIE: E-mail?

WILBUR: No.

WINNIE: Too bad. Spell book please.

WILBUR: Fetch it yourself. I'm going to write to Mogg again and I'm going to tell him either he wants to be friends or –

WINNIE fetches her large spell book. Clicking her tongue and grinding her teeth as she searches for a spell. WILBUR starts to write a letter.

Dear Mogg –

WINNIE: (*Reading.*) Here we are. How to conjure a Summer's Day. Think of, and line up in your mind, in order of preference, seven sunny summer days you have enjoyed in the past however many summers you've lived. Only one day per summer. If you can't think of seven, because you're under seven years old, just think of your favourite summer's day…ever. Where were you? Who were you with? What were you doing? This will be easy if your birthday's in the summer. Which mine is.

WILBUR: (*Writing.*) How are you? I'm okay.

WINNIE: (*Reading.*) Now think of seven of the coldest, wettest, frosty snow-bound winter days… Or one if you're under seven. Where were you? Who were you with? What were you doing?

WILBUR: (*Writing.*) Did you get my letter?

WINNIE: (*Reading.*) Place the fourteen, or two days on top of each other and subtract the feelings you have for the winter from the summer. In other words if what you were doing, who you were doing it with, and where you were doing it, would have been improved by the weather being good – who writes this stuff? – then you have more positive feelings about the summer than winter. You're a summer person.

WILBUR: (*Writing.*) E-mail?

WINNIE: (*Reading.*) I'm a summer person.

WILBUR: (*Writing.*) If you don't reply to this letter, I take it we're not friends anymore.

WINNIE: (*Reading.*) Now, whilst you're thinking about summer. Put on a pair of sunglasses. Rub the remains of last years sun lotion on your arms, skip and don't drag your feet, greet every living creature with a smile, take your time with everything, and sigh contentedly at regular intervals. (*She tries.*) Ahhh! This is what some call sympathetic magic and has a hundred per cent success rate. Armed with your thoughts, actions and props wave your wand with the hand you write with. Be sure to wave your wand in an anticlockwise direction. If you don't you may conjure a more severe winter than the one you are currently experiencing and be frozen alive like many an Antarctic explorer.

WILBUR: (*Writing.*) Lots of love…

WINNIE: (*Reading.*) Speak the thought. Wave the wand.

WILBUR: (*Signing off.*) Wilbur.

Music 32.

WINNIE comes into the garden. Followed by WILBUR.

COMB: Hi, Winnie! It's freezing, isn't it?

All shiver.

WINNIE: I'm going to make summer. I'm thinking I'm
sitting in a deck chair in the garden...without my socks
on...one thought – whoosh! (*Waves wand.*) Sucking an ice
cream sundae through a stripey straw... (*Waves wand.*)
Grapes and grapefruit to hand... (*Waves wand.*) Tickling
my favourite cat, that's you, Wilbur, on your back, soft
and purring ... (*Waves wand.*) The sound of the bees, the
smell of the grass, reading a copy *Witch's Weekly.*
Abracadabra!

Music 33.

*WINNIE waves her wand and suddenly the garden is full of
summer. The floor is unfurled to reveal sprung flowers, the
body of the snowman is removed to reveal a large cauldron
filled with ice and cans of drink, white cloths are removed to
reveal a deck chair etc.*

ALL: Here comes summer!

Music 34. 'Song of Summer.'

We'll sing you a song of summer,
When the nights are short and the days are long,
When the skies are clear and the birds in song
We'll sing you a song of summer.

In the hazy sweet heat flowers grow and unfurl
Drowsy animals wake to explore a new world,
Busy bees buzz by in search of a treat
While little lambs bleat and foals find their feet.

We'll sing you a song of summer,
When the nights are short and the days are long,

When the skies are clear and the birds in song
We'll sing you a song of summer.

WINNIE: Let's have a deck chair, and a cauldron of ice
Cool drinks and a rug by the pond would be nice
While I tan this body, sleep under my seat,
But when I rub your sleek fur you must massage my feet.

ALL: Ah! Oooooooo!
Ah! Oooooooo!
Relaxxxxxxx!   ·
Sing me a song of summer.

WILBUR: Miaowwwww!

SNAKE: In the middle of summer, my new skin won't keep
It's a long spring I need to get used to this heat.
It's cracking and peeling, and I'm in such pain,
Let me sleep in the cold, let me shower in the rain.

FLOWERS: Our petals are bleached, and our roots are sore,
We're so tired and droopy, can't grow anymore
We need a good rest, to restore our allure,
Please let us hide down in the ground like before

ALL: We'll sing you a song of summer,
When the nights are short and the days are long,
When the skies are clear and the birds in song
We'll sing you a song of summer.

SNOUT: There's a restless big crowd, lining up at your gate,
They want a bit of summer and say they won't wait,
They've suffered their winter for quite long enough
If we don't let them in they'll start getting rough.

WINNIE: They're all welcome in for a mid winter swim,
For a picnic and a jive, friends! – you're all welcome in!
You can fly your kites you can play volley ball,
But keep your hands off my wand I implore.

ALL: We'll sing you a song of summer
When the nights are short and the days are long,
When the skies are clear and the birds in song
We'll sing you a song of summer.

Ah! Oooooooo!
Ah! Oooooooo!
We'll sing you a song of summer,
Relaxxxxxxx!
Sing me a song of summer.

Audience members are invited onto the stage. They are encouraged to play a game (skittles, catch, whatever) with the actors. Improvise. The actors orchestrate the audience.

As the stage fills with people the music continues. Puppets and people mingle. WINNIE loses WILBUR. She searches for him, high and low.

WINNIE: Excuse me, has anyone seen Wilbur? Excuse me... (*Etc.*)

WILBUR is seen across a crowded garden on someone's shoulders

Wilbur! Wilbur! Come here! Quickly before I lose you.

WILBUR makes his way back to WINNIE, but he is distracted by the crowd.

Wilbur come here before I lose you forever. There are too many people here, Wilburn! Making too much noise. I can't hear to see you, Wilbur. I can't relax. People making too much mess. I'm not changing my garden black and falling over you again. This lovely bit of summer is turning out horrible. Come back, Winter!

The sound of an ice cream van approaching.

WILBUR: I want an ice cream. Winnie, can I have one?

WINNIE: (*Furious.*) No one sells ice cream in my garden! No one!

WILBUR: Please Winnie. I never had one in India.

WINNIE: No, Wilbur. (*Stamping her foot, furiously, she waves her wand.*) Abracadabra!

Music 35.

The snow starts to fall. Summer disappears as quickly as it was created, and winter returns. The stage is cleared. The last to leave is SNAKE...very, very slowly.

WINNIE and WILBUR return to the kitchen. It's warm and snug. In silence WINNIE offers WILBUR a saucer of milk. WILBUR refuses.

Wilbur I'm sorry you couldn't have an ice cream. If you had had one they'd all have had to have one. Think how long you'd have had to have queued. Imagine the state of the garden with all those wrappers on the ground.

WILBUR sulks.

I hate to see you miserable. You know I do.

She sits down to read her book. Catches sight of a letter on the floor.

When did this arrive? It's for you Wilbur. It's from Australia.

She opens it and hands it to him.

WILBUR reads it in silence.

It's warm in here, don't you think? Cosy with just the two of us.

WILBUR: Mogg says he's going to stow away on the next ship to England.

WILBUR settles on WINNIE's lap.

WINNIE: That's good news, isn't it, Wilbur? He'll have to come and stay. Cheer up. The creatures have all gone back to bed to finish their winter sleep; the flowers back underground to wait for spring. If you like, Wilbur, you can sleep on my bed tonight.

Music 36. 'A Cat in a Million' (Reprise).

ALL: He's a cat in a million, he's sleek cool and wise,
With his elegant fur and his emerald green eyes,
Oh, what must she do to make him realise
Every moment she's with him, life's a surprise.

The End